POPPY'S DAY
— at the —
AQUARIUM

By Rachel Cherry
Illustrated by Laraib I. Sukhera

Aquarium

This book is dedicated to my lovely friend Marin.
You are growing up so fast, and I hope you read
this book and have a laugh with me.
Many blessings, my sweet girl.

Poppy's Day at the Aquarium
Copyright 2022 by Rachel Cherry | instagram.com/wercherries
Illustrated by Laraib I. Sukhera
Published by Argyle Fox Publishing | argylefoxpublishing.com
ISBN 978-1-953259-49-3 (Paperback)
ISBN 978-1-953259-48-6 (Hardcover)

There once was a little girl named Poppy. She had yellow ringlets of hair that fell down her back.

Poppy loved playing dress-up.
She loved going out with Aunt Lucy
even more.

On summer break, Aunt Lucy planned an adventure with Poppy. They would spend the day at the aquarium.

Poppy felt like the luckiest girl in the world!

As soon as Poppy walked into the aquarium, the flamingos greeted her.

"Hey," Poppy said, "I know those guys. They're pink flamingos!"

Aunt Lucy asked if Poppy knew how to say *pink* in Spanish.

Poppy thought for a moment.

"*Rosado!*" she said. "That's my favorite color. I love anything that's *rosado!*"

Aunt Lucy smiled.

"Where do you think the clownfish is today?" Aunt Lucy asked. "I love clowns." Poppy pointed to Mr. Henry. "Let's ask him," she said. "He'll know!"

Mr. Henry explained that the clownfish is one of the most popular fish at the aquarium. He often hides though, because he's a little shy.

In fact, he was probably hiding at that moment.

"Mr. Henry's shirt is *green*." Poppy closed one eye to think. "That's *verde* in Spanish. Right, Aunt Lucy?"

"Good job, Poppy. Do you know how to say *fish* in Spanish?"
"Yes, Aunt Lucy! It's *pescado*!"

Mr. Henry shuffled to Poppy's side. He leaned down and nodded to Poppy's left.

"Here we have a *tortuga*," he said. "Do you know what that means?"

"I do!" Poppy said. "*Tortuga* means *turtle*. He has a hard shell."

Mr. Henry patted Poppy on the head. "You're a smart girl," he said. "The shell protects this *tortuga* from predators. Oh— and did you know that turtles love to eat fruit?"

Poppy licked her lips. She loved fruit too!

When Poppy and Aunt Lucy went to see the dolphins, Mr. Henry explained that they have two stomachs.

"Grandma must have two stomachs also," Poppy said. "She eats two full plates at Sunday dinner, and I can barely finish one!"

"Dolphins don't just eat a lot," Mr. Henry laughed. "They can live for fifty years, and they love to stay with their mommies."

Poppy loved that idea. "*Madres*," she told Mr. Henry. "Dolphins love to stay with their *madres!*"

The penguins were next. Mr. Henry said that they're great swimmers who stay with their mates for life. They're also like little kids. They love sliding down the ice, over and over.

Poppy leaned toward Aunt Lucy.
"They are *negro y blanco*," she said.
"That means *black and white*!"

Aunt Lucy looked impressed. Then she looked at her watch. "Poppy," she said, "where has the day gone? It's already time to say goodbye to the aquarium and thank you to Mr. Henry!"

"*Adios, amigos!*" Poppy called to her aquarium friends. "*Muchas gracias, Sr. Henry!*"

As they drove home in Aunt Lucy's convertible, Poppy's hair blew in the wind.

"Aunt Lucy," Poppy said, "What color is my hair in Spanish?"

"The same color as the sun," Aunt Lucy replied.

"*Yellow!*" Poppy said, raising both hands overhead. "That's *amarillo* in Spanish!"

When Poppy got home, she opened her front door and got a big surprise.

"HAPPY BIRTHDAY!"

Poppy put her hands over her mouth. Her mother held a huge birthday cake.

Balloons bounced and floated across the room. Family and friends clapped and smiled at Poppy.

"You're five now," Aunt Lucy whispered. "Happy birthday!" She handed Poppy a fishbowl with a shiny blue fish in it.

Poppy hugged Aunt Lucy and thanked her over and over and over again.
"So," Aunt Lucy said, "what are you going to name your new fish?"

Poppy squinted at the fish. She looked at the ceiling, thinking. Finally, she had a name: *"Rojo Gato."*

"*Red Cat?*" Aunt Lucy scratched her head. "Why do you want to name your blue fish *Red Cat?*"

Poppy didn't answer. She just laughed and laughed.

CPSIA information can be obtained
at www.ICGtesting.com
Printed in the USA
BVHW020735251122
652754BV00008B/79